GW01079956

BETWEEN TH
AND
OTHER PC

BETWEEN THE ACTS
and other poems

Cyril Cusack

COLIN SMYTHE
Gerrards Cross, 1990

Copyright © 1970, 1990 by Cyril Cusack

This collection first published in 1990 by Colin Smythe Limited,
Gerrards Cross, Buckinghamshire

British Library Cataloguing in Publication Data

Cusack, Cyril 1910–
Between the acts and other poems.
I. Title
823.914

ISBN 0–86140–332–0

ISBN 0–86140–332–0

Printed and bound in Great Britain
by Dotesios Printers Ltd, Trowbridge, Wiltshire.

TO THE COMPANY

ACKNOWLEDGEMENTS

To the editors of *Commonweal, The Genesian, The Irish Press,The Irish Times, The London Magazine, The Month, The New York Times, The Spectator, The Tablet, The Times* and *The Transatlantic Review.*

Some of these poems first appeared in *Timepieces* (Dublin: The Dolmen Press, 1970).

CONTENTS

TO ELIZABETH IN ROME

Words Horace wrote
Complaining of his love-sick friends —
'Oh, how may I write poetry in Rome?'
And if not Horace who then can?
Shall I, an Irish nanny-goat,
Bleat louder when his own verse blends
Much less with Dante Alighieri than
With some aspiring Chesterton?
Or, willy-nilly, in another town
Dare fill with silly frilly lines a tome?

This 'other son' —
For so she named me — well held down
in Rome's deep anchorage of bells,
Half-blinded by the light from Peter's dome,
Half-murdered in my soul now torn
Into innumerable hells
Between La Lupa and the Shrew,
May I not, even in expiring breath,
Yet speak a true love, utter true-
Born poetry in just . . . 'Elizabeth!'?

FROM LYME REGIS TO AN ACTRESS

O joyous swoop of field down Devonside
and trooping eye-blue flax, white-headed tide
by Golden Cap, the Golden Cap at Lyme;
and Dorset lanes with honeysuckle, thyme

and cowslip sweetnesses attract
the heart, enticing it towards those
secrets hidden in the heart of time
while bidding riddle yield, retract
in timelessness, but none heart knows
so sweet as budding English rose.

A blossoming too late for me, a high-born
one I cannot tread or trip upon,
yet she, fair rarest budding rose,
can reach the heart, can heart enclose,
entrap, have stripe and strip upon
the rose's thorn, the rose's thorn.

But since I cannot have her queen
me, she who that sweet other is
who could not otherwise have been,
nor princess be, for that be she
who still in bud, alas, is his,
another's — yet another he!

The Queen-in-Waiting let her be,
O fairest little English rose,
for other years than her nineteen
Pretender be — I name her Jean —
until the heart in time enclose
the riddle, riddle open rose to me.

ADORABLE DIVA

Puccini's most darling Butterfly —
thrice silent nor the fluttering fan
on stage in your Opera House, Milan,
when you of the soaring feather voice
caught in the throat that McSwiney should die
stopped for country you could not work
the scene. And now, dear Margaret Burke
Sheridan, could we not but rejoice
gladdened in memory — Butterfly feet
a twinkle down a grey Dublin street.

"OUR MAN IN TUNIS"

(for Zeffirelli)

He is totally untroubled and untrammeled
By emotional disturbances and stress,
Your companionable valuable camel
We have reason to perpetually bless;
For quite obviously the reason must be this:
Due, less charitably speaking, to the fewness
(No, no *verbum non Romanum* to dismiss!)
Of more palatable animals in Tunis.

ESCAPE LINES
FROM Zeffirelli's Jesus of Nazareth

Here underneath this sandy mound
Somebody's body may be found,
Remains remain — I trust not mine,
However deadly undivine! —
That failed to toe the Roman line.
(That doctrine, was it ever sound,
To have us buried underground?)
So please you, am I out of line,
Sir, in maintaining my design
To meet my Maker homeward bound!

THE OLD QUEEN'S, DUBLIN

Fingers like withering flowers fall
over the worn fibred places of a shawl
teasing the strands;

draping
sudden laughter with hands,
scraping wet butts at a wall,
cursing, calling a name,
rehearsing sad scenes —
outside the old Queen's,
dry weather and wet
these
play the game,
the same game of self-please,
strut and fret;

a xylophone's
stutter, the tones
of the queue where it stands
shuffling —
a mask and a marionette —
or gutter-wise leans
snuffling
at a warm coat's breath —
these at a shake of the bones
form the old, the same
make-believe shibboleth.

THE TOUR

1

"Before you were born
I was dancing, my dear,
in revue — *The Gay Gordons*;
my hair was the colour of corn,
and my hair, it swung down
all the way, down to here —
and everyone said it was gorgeous —

" 'splits' and high kicks
in the very front row of the chorus —
at Cambridge the fellows flung down
from the gallery
rosetted garters and flowers —
with *Sir* Seymour Hicks
and on quite a nice salary.

"And then were the tours
in the 'fit-ups' — Boucicault
with the 'legits' . . . *Arrah-na-Pogue*
and *The Colleen Bawn*
and my 'Isabel' too, in lovely *East Lynne* —
oh, before you were born —
and still they will tell you in Tarbet and Glin
how the audience cried
every night when I sobbed
as sweet 'Little Willie', he died.

"My hair I had bobbed
and dyed red for our rep.
in Dear Dirty Dublin, the Queen's;
McShane was the fireman
there on the dress-circle step;
houses twice-nightly, between
them at Jammet's — an unknown admirer —
the high standing dinner — no strings attached;
and the old orange-sellers, they always latched
on to me, cheered me on sight
down the lane to the stage-door each night. . ."

THE TOUR

2

But now — change of scene
and of make-up — old girl, bless her heart,
partly bald under wisps of white hair —
not a wig, sir — she still swigs a drop
of neat whisky in this her last character part,
stumping around on a stick for a prop.
More often she squats in a bumpy wheelchair,
whiskery, broke, deaf and arthritic . . .
But posing the mask
yet again, she can yell — "Oh, that blasted critic!"
or "Who is he, tell us, the newest lover?
Come on, what's the gossip?' she'll sharply ask —
although the dance, the tour is over.

LAMENT FOR OLD LADIES

Have we left the old ladies,
left them behind,
have we lost them, bereaving
them tossed into Hades
and leaving them thus
forever left grieving
bereft of dear us?
I mean, have we been kind?

Tall islander Peig by a darkening hearth
who called up her saga from heart of the earth;
Mrs P-hyphen-A, beached close to the sea,
in full beaded blouse and the pleated skirt
to greet Admiral son — and terriers three,
a dumpy bundle of dignity
proffering gins with a syphon squirt
or else at low tide pale afternoon tea;

then gay Mrs Comerford — "No heavy load,
all seventeen kids . . .", or so she would say
freed from her muddle of widow's weeds,
still sturdily smiling, her week's holiday
at far Kilmacanogue (a mile up the road)
with 'relations'. Now in what comfort she feeds
herself only — a cross — whatever the catch.

See squinting to count what's left in the box
a North London granny scratching a match —
she waddled through wars under hundreds of shocks
and thick yellow fogs and her peace-time fears
to squeeze with a wheeze into ninety-eight years;
while her chorus-girl daughter last courted by death
kept playing it up to her dying breath;

'Ma' Kelly, game gossip on one gammy leg,
non-stop or non-starter, just anxious to please,
yet proud, never stooping, no, never, to beg;
last, Nell low domestic, a tremble, half-blind
and heaven-high smelling of some odd disease,
rooting around, half out of her mind. . .

and so on and so on,
all old ladies, old ladies unsung
past retrieving,
all done with — 'Well done!'

Is it we should be grieving
believing them gone,
only they who were young
of another kind
who have left, only us left behind?

ON THE DEATH OF AN OLD CHORUS GIRL

Of days of high kicks, splits,
of garters, of galleryites,
of plush and gilt, a certain grace
in stalls where grace no longer sits,
of 'digs', late boats and gayest nights —
here she of 'once upon a time'
lies still and with white marbled face
called from 'the good old days' to this
her last . . . but here the chrysalis,
and might I see a butterfly
push out its wings and climb
from that old skin and fly.

TO A DEAD COMEDIAN

It was a rough day,
a rough day for a burial,
wet. Blustering wind, rain
left small time for sentiment. Pain
of a lost merriment — unusual —

attended the comedian's funeral,
his going down. Our man
of our town, turning his head away
from tedium in game refusal
had ended much as he began.

God knows his creature,
knows the uncommon clown in each of us.
But is it not a tough old station
where laughter may be medium for grief
and Death be seen, a common thief,

stealing the tag and leaving us —
on-stage — the rag for compensation
and a chief player with no line to say.
It was a rough day,
a rough day for the theatre.

THE TIVOLI, DUBLIN

Pressing
the gallery pored
with stopped faces.

Dressing-
room number? Miss . . . ?
Yes, sir!
She signs them a kiss,
light and furrow change places,
and changing — the terpsichord.

Near one who is dead now, who snored
stirring wet moustaches,
through slumbrous lashes
one who is dead
stared down at a maid — pale thread
of silk swaying, frail chord
of a theme lightly played, lightly scored.

POSTSCRIPT TO PLAYBOY

Randy Sarah Tansy, Honor Blake
and — what's-her-name — the other pearl,
girls who, for Christy Mahon's sake,
would all too soon have gone to hell,
to end it took, assumed the veil —
what else should Gaelic lassies take? —
and Playboy lost, none left to tell
of how the heart, although a wonder —
as the full pack, all four suits fell —
too easily may fall asunder,
they now regale the bloody tale
in cloistered tones, one to another.
Small blame, but Pity, ring the bell,
for Pegeen Mike's the Reverend Mother!

O'CASEY REJECT

The Bishop's Bonfire (Gaiety Theatre, Dublin,
28 February 1955, Cyril Cusack Productions).

O there he is that never took a hint,
your greyhaired squinting squire at seventy-four
beneath her window's shuteyed firmament
still firmly rat-tat-tattin' at her door.

The Lady — lady now, no less — says "No!",
as once her oul' one said the same before.
Who'd blame him so, hard rooted heel and toe
sent reeling, calling her a little whore?

"Hey, who's that rat-tat-tattin' at me door,
kickin' up a holy shindy? Is it you,
ye back-street number? Seventy-four —
at your age knockin', what ye'd die to do!"

Where e'er she walks with hairy airs, a pose
for hawkin' round unwearables, new wares
for old, her hoity-toity talkin' shows
her careless of unbearably sad cares.

"And who's that rat-tat-tattin' at me door,
shakin' me achin' acres yet again
that's decent and respectable — what's more,
delectable, say all those writin' men?

"Before a spout of Dublin blood is shed,
ye red-eyed drip of Beelzebub, ye lout,
one word — ye heard what the Old Lady said —
it's 'NO!', ye get, get out and stay out — OUT!"

LAMENT FOR THEATRE

Once matchless image and now broken,
hatcheted about by light-
-o'-loves, if she snatches at some token
of old glory in the night,
her swan-song sung, what little city
is is pitches at her pretty feet
its single coin of jingling pity
which is no more than counterfeit!

MELODRAMA

I walked the grave main street
of a winter date, a seaside town
at night dreaming — dreaming
the curtain might not yet be down —
the play by Boucicault —
all a seeming, seeming
but a yesternight of fifty years ago
when I might reach the hall to greet
the gret O'Rorke, actor they well know
for his last curtain speech — proud ghost
costumed still as Shaun the Post.

Torn playbill fluttering on the wall
says that, following Arrah-na-pogue,
the play will be, at the town hall,
none other than The Colleen Bawn
with the O'Rorke as ragged rogue
Myles vagabond, our hero rake.

But now no posters up, no bellman ringing
to tell of Myles-na-gCopaleen swinging
perilously across Killarney lake
to Eily's rescue from the hunchback, Danny Mann —
and not for Hardress Cregan's sake —
for Myles, he loves her as no other can . . .
No oil-lamps lighting up the scene
on scamp beloved, Myles-na-gCopaleen.

I walked the grave main street
of a seaside town, straying, straying
as once I did a full half-century ago
to see my father bravely playing, playing
those parts in Boucicault — but 'One Week
Only'. Must I now give up my seat,
a complimentary, to take the blow
of wintry wind on wrinkled cheek
and brow, allowing it to fade,
my dream down empty esplanade?

TRESPASS

They say in Meath the Tinkerboy's a fright
for noise, and that's no lie, by everything.
If God gave me the strength — as well He might —
to squeeze in easy on an eagle's wing
and whizz across the dizzy gap of night
as far as the White Courtyard, there I'd sing
hard by the gate a song Himself could smile
at — had Himself a mind to — not a hymn
but a thing, hell's bells, you could hear a mile
away from Limbo — aye, from Kells to Trim —
a tinker tune with jizz in it, a swing.
God knows, they might not like that sort of thing.

With strength of wing and limb I'd take a chance
on that itself, for by my soul, it's sad
to think they're half the time in half a trance.
I'd bawl it out to beat the band, by Dad,
to see old Paradise up prancing in a dance,
once in the lengthy span they have go mad
with laughing maybe, and the holy saints
all cutting capers on the golden floor.
With dust and stuff there might be odd complaints
I wouldn't hold on long outside the door,
for after all the fun they would have had
they might be hard on a poor tinker lad.

'SHAUGHRAUN'

Eisean ag siúil na mbóthar 'sa' choinfheascar,
é loithte le h-uaigneas ar thóir ar an gcroí,
duine is fearr leis go mór 'bheith mi-sheascair.
Ach cé h-é an fáth — é 'n a sheachránuí?

Súilí na cathrach a's iad ag lonnradh
gan chaitheamh aon tsoluis ar thuras an chroi,
súilí na h-óiche nách nochtann ach scannradh
an domhain dó choiche — do'n tseachránuí . . .

Buaileadh na fearthainne ar an tsean-thalamh
a's dúlaitheach aigne, ualach ar chroi,
múchta an teine, an teach dúnta falamh —
A's 'tuige na béadh se 'n a sheachránuí?

THE SHAUGHRAUN[1]

Going all roads in the last of the light,
lost and alone in his own heart's maze
and making for choice his own unease —
whither and why that wandering flight?

City-eyes lit from the lie of the sun
throwing no light on the heart's road here
and night-eyes knowing the naked fear
in him always, the wandering one . . .

Dimming the hearth-fire, latched the door,
and bitter the rain down that old, old road
with dullness of mind from his own heart's load —
why would he not be a wanderer?

[1] Translation of previous poem.

FEAR AN-IOMAD GHRÁDHA

Ar thaoibh thall an bhóthair a thuit me mi-shásta
    Is tá rómham geal-ghúna na spéire mar shíoda
'S mion-chraobhógai na gcrann a's iad mar dhú-lása
    A's an-iomad ghrádha laistigh i mo chroi-se.

Mhuise, 'tuige a mbím-se annso i mo shui-se?
    An-iomad ghrádha 'ionnam a chuir orm an t-uaigneas;
A's ceannacha bhána chím i measc na gcraobhán —
    Sid iad aghaidh na ndaoine nár chorrui chun fáin;

Aghaidhe 'ta ruicneach, duilleóga 'sa' bhFómhair
    A'ss iad ar ti tuitim anuas ar cham-bhóithribh,
Aghaidhe 'ta caillte uaim — ná ni orm-sa an locht —
    A's suidhim annsúd ar mo chroi-bhacach bhocht.

THE LOVE MAN

Translated from the poem 'Fear an-iomad Ghradha'.

Far side of a ditch there I fell into sadness,
the skein of wild silk above stretched out before me
— a sigh from the core of the woman that bore me —
with love overcome and a sure sign of madness.

What hold is it has me here squatting half-murdered
but love and a web of grey faces unworded,
the leaf-lace of other lost autumns astray
in my head, till they break into dust blown away

to a long reach of road in a twist where it parts
us to leave me lamenting, a beggar of hearts.
I sit on the ditch so, for all ye may see,
and woefully wonder whose fault could it be.

TINKER'S GIRL

O we had travelled the hard roads
    The little one and I,
When the roads were hard and frosted,
    The dark-haired one and I.
O we had spoken the bitter words
    And I had made her cry . . .
Though my love she had no beauty
    O I wished that I might die.

I have sauntered down the valleys
    With other ones, have I;
I have kissed along the wood-paths
    Where the beech-leaves lie
Shifting like distant whispers . . .
    O the other ones may sigh,
They may have all summer's beauty,
    Yet for them I would not die.

And now I have lost the dark one . . .
    Though bitter blue her eye
O I would wish for the hard roads
    And the little one close by.
Though my mouth be emptied of kisses
    And ten ones have sauntered by,
O now I have lost my only one
    I wish that I might die.

LOVE IN EXILE

My world be yours,
all — all that is in Ireland here,
the rainful gorse,
grasses gliding upon a weir,
air hay-honeyed from rain,
hills the late light has lain
on and shall lie again;

old trees that fade
in slow mist drifted from the sea —
these from my shade,
and all rich things I cannot see,
all rich things you forsook,
I give you, seeking as I look
for you, all else you took.

PROCESSIONAL

. . . and you from the tall ragged house in the Square,
I like how you dance.
For you move like top cedar-boughs swayed in a wind,
and you move like spray fanned from the top of the sea,
and your hair is a deep river falling apart under night.
I might like how you dance —
in your eye is the shine of green marble, of rock.

There is you, whose soft hair
is a cloud, cloud at evening
after the sun,
I have seen, at white morning
astir behind spruce and fir;
secretly shifting
like morning itself behind leaves
I have seen you up to your knees
in the deep deep bronze
of a pool on Djouce Mountain.
You smile — but your smile is the softness of lake-sand.

There is you from whose eyes
flutter butterflies winking bright wings in the forenoon,
you who have seen yellow mansions
over the distance of long London parks,
through the stems of stilled beeches,
of elm and wide chestnut, start
brightening, and people flitting along behind railings.
You who have seen the yellow moon torn
amid London house-tops,
did I ever blame you for wanting to fly
to where the sun is still warm?

I shall go then to her, my birch sapling
that leans by a river — the salmon-streaked Easkey —
hides slyly away from me, silver-shade lady . . .
at day-break to meet a shy greeting of leaves
and to kiss the wet bark.

And shall she then, but she, be my bride?
Shall we wed then when I . . . I am Dead?

LAST LOVE

In this my old time of loving
I could wish to have you lie
here beneath my willow, moving
as slim minnow-lights fly by.

I would have you see, dear worlding —
not much further than your nose —
that the light picks out quick bird-wing
is all love God only knows.

And I wish, when you are winking
out your twentieth-century mood,
you would trace His wishful thinking
in the bark of my old wood.

NATAL SNAPSHOT — 1904

You throw down your challenge and I accept,
policeman there, mounted, moustached and so
so proud of the three fat stripes you show.
Would I only babble the faith you kept?

Recall, sir, the veldt and, nodding two-deep,
that well-belted son of a Boer, a defeat,
with you, saddle-sore, shagged, deadbeat,
the bandoliered shoulder you fell to for sleep;

the fable you told me — black Jesus' birth
and the pillaged stable. Oh, I can be roused
and matter to me that you now lie housed
ill-at-ease with your brothers in African earth.

Yes, I can be proud of your squireen pose,
the loud enough stripes, full cuffs and all,
of you who once caught me about to fall,
once taught me to run pell-mell on my toes.

TO PADRAIG, NEWBORN

Marchtossed, darkdowned son —
more than myself and beyond
my father's needle eye
I see in you — accuser friend,
forgiving enemy —
each passerby;

see everyone —
beggar, poet; the hard
and fast tycoon,
boor, chancer, Jew dejected;
poor hopeless soak, another
character and card,
buffoon;

or possibly lay-brother,
cardinal maybe,
or even Pope
in smoke elected.
And in your lolling head I see
at once both lawyer wrangling
and criminal rejected
dangling
on a rope;

or sent to mend the sick,
some dedicated;
saint in ecstasy
or crazy-gazing lunatic;

and, if some part of me,
yet something of her womanhood
who stands where Mary stood
and waited,
sword in heart,
who, seeing you the thief on either side,
sees more, sees you to be
in these a part
of the still Crucified.

RETROSPECT

He watched those great men going up the stairs
latching on to shiny bannisters,
ascending, gravely climbing men unmatched
in ways — in ways. At foot of the stairs detached,
somehow bereft, not lost but left, his tears
dried funded a smiling sixpence, small in years
he watched those trousered legs uplift
theatrically, lacking but the actor's gift,
up the soft-carpeted anglo-Irish stairs,
a silent striving — preparatory prayers —
men Treaty-bound observing a new grace
in leadership of an old, a bleeding race,
relieved for the country to be still alive.
He stared and stared, for he was only five.

"Say, little black one, sitting there
with Mammy in the tube aware —
yes, even without seeming to —
of people when they stare and stare
at you the rude way that they do,
now tell me truly, do you care?"

"Oh, well I know my face is black,
still blacker under my white cap,
and you can think I wouldn't dare
as hard as stone to stare them back
as hard as they — for I could trap
them with my eye and catch them out.

"You see that cagey customer,
the fellow with the dirty leer.
What would that white man be about —
not to embrace me but to strangle?

"I'm not afraid, what should I fear
with my Big Mammy sitting here
beside me, strong, big-boned and stout
and dangling on her wrist her bangle.

"My Mammy has a wary eye
and I can tell you truly, sir,
my Mammy keeps a sharp look out.
But, sir, why do they stare so, why?"

WHEN YOU WERE SIX

The days of gold, my love, roll by
in rigmarole from day to day,
and never should we wonder why
they turn to silver on the way
to God knows where. (Or is it fair
that no-one knows the way to Where?)

And never, now you are aged six,
O never must they turn to lead:
and though not high enough to mix
with those who talk above our head
who, when we plead — 'Please talk to us!'
or 'Mummy, what was that you said?'
make such a loud unearthly fuss
and tartly tell us, 'Time for bed!',

find time we can, we *must* find time
for you and me to play the game
(it may not always be the same),
and who shall say it is a crime
to rescue Hiawatha just in time
to stay that villain, Buff'lo Bill
(played brutally by me)
from roping Hiawatha, you
around the jacaranda tree
away up there on that thar hill
which is — I know you know it's true —
the sofa by the window-sill.

Remember that Big Chief — B.C.?
Aye, very ancient, almost bent
(a secondary role for me),
by this time (bed-time!) slightly doped
and swaying in his arm-chair tent
from all that firewater, who —
however pie-eyed — still could see
both far and wide and through and through
binoculars our Redskin roped
fast to that jacaranda tree.

Cried he, 'Black Feather and Red Foot,
untether all the horses, *but*

be careful not to shoot to kill
that awful b — , old Buff'lo Bill!
Just ride like mad across the plain
(plain carpet), track him down again!'

Well, surely here's the final test:
at Hiawatha's own request
the bold B.B. was let go free
and spared a fiery inquest,
spared all unnecessary pain
to range those purple hills again . . .
entirely at her best,
our daring Princess of the plain.

So who shall say that it is sin
to let the years of gold roll by
in rigmarole? Or who shall say
the game is over or I lie
that she'll return in fair red skin
to play again another day!

INFANT DIALOGUE

(at Westminster Cathedral)

ON THE NEW LITURGY

'Oh, what a lot of portions!', looking up at me
she said. 'Well, yes,' I said. What could I but agree?
'The Lord, he is my Portion,' the Chosen Ones, yes, we
responded with appropriate solemnity.

(*'Good Lord, how could the Good Lord so divided be!'*)
'You're looking awful gloomy. Come on, smile,' said she.
I smiled a smile. That's better, — and then guilelessly
she added, 'Well, He *is* Almighty, isn't he!'

ON PENANCE

'I am a little naughty, I am a little good.'
(*and that quite clearly must be clearly understood —
our poor humanity's peculiar condition*)
'And so, dear child, repeat — I *know* you said you would,
my sweet! — that old imperfect Act of mild Contrition. . .
What's that! And so should I, you say! You *know* I should?'

THE GOLDEN OWL OF ORKNEY (1)

The Golden Owl of Orkney
glared far out to sea.
He'd heard the King of Norway
was visiting in May.

The Golden Owl of Orkney,
he winked an eye at me:
'O I could tell a tale or two —
right well I could!' says he.

Is he not a noble laird,
the very last might be?
Many a whisper has he heard
high up his twiggy tree.

'When comes that loafing Olaf,
O will I squark and boo!
I, Golden Owl of Orkney,
I'll howl — TU-WHIT, TU-WHO!'

THE GOLDEN OWL OF ORKNEY (2)

In Orkney sits a Golden Owl
who blinks and winks and thinks he thinks —
of mists and moons and murder foul
in dungeons dark in the presincts

of ghosty towers where nightly flits —
who years ago to Burray fled —
that heady waiter from the Ritz
who lost his head and bled and bled.

But truth to tell, on wiry fence
that Golden Owl alone still sits
all tense in this immense pretense
and scares himself out of his wits.

In Orkney squats that Golden Owl
and makes — in fact, he *is* — a howl.

LONDON SPRING

O London looked lovely on the Sunday
she rode through the streets so gaily
down lavender ways that were muted
in morning, threaded into one way
awaiting that gossamer lady
riding by brick and blossom, her beauty
shaming the scavenger shade, the
sad shadow still lingering palely.

O London looked lovely on that Sunday
awakening from dream to the glory
of the little aristocrat tossing
her silver to all and sundry.
By squares, windows and balconies crowded
with golden history, crossing
from view down a mews she proudly
saluted the old and the new story.

THE CAPITAL

And whereto now do I belong,
this pilgrim player?
No longer to a city where
to rowdy rhythm, overcrowding song
they grovel, grope, grapple, grab
myopic toward the mortuary slab.

Not there —
your Lilliput built up to monster height —
not there but where
at fairytime no substitute for Right
was Wrong
nor curse for prayer.

Man, no more kneel and play
the grand Amen
at this land's altar, probe
the tabernacle is He there,
still there, not gone from men
away,

drained dry upon a cross
leading the great escape
from a dead loss,
not gone from me.
Pray light from night, enough to see
is the white missionary's robe

cloaking a second flight
from rape
in another Herod's sight.
Or long ago did He just take
shape when a Patrick came to boss
the land — in guise of snake?

VIEWS FROM A BICYCLE

Alongside highup houseproud houses
heavyeyed dressed up in county
graces, hobbles Silverfoot with bounty
to where Sandymount carouses.

Dear Dodder water dawdling down,
old dodderer, go paddle in the sea.
But should that truant tiddler be
dodging back to Dublin Town?

Two joyous cycling girls, one
calling saucyvoiced in flight,
'And there was me a holy sight . . .'
skirts blowing, boisterously gone.

Gone flying pretty petticoats,
no wriggling tiddler should have sinned
against the tide — but wags what wind
to riddle out black sheep from goats?

Her lover over, blousily
there fingering a daisychain
miss calculates the kiss checkmating.
Cat or mouse — who fiddles free?
Will others lie where miss has lain
in wait with all her lacy baiting?

So — push your pedal, contemplating
who may crush the rebel grain.

VOCATION: 1940–1970

Somewhere in the Underground
of War we wound
up, in the backwoods of battle bored
with it all and each other and bound
to be talking of Ireland, applauding the Cause,
quite regardless of wars
or acts of the Lord
and sudden bombs falling.

The dull sullen thunders of war
half-recalling,
I recollect now a spoiled nun
somehow foiled in her calling.
Despoiled of her fun,
now become more than ever a bore
she collects from the poor
for a church in the new Ballymun.

THE FALL

Let pass
the old autumnal
stroller going going gone
to grass
to go to earth, to seed.
Why stay with sentiment,

delay
for rider on late steed
or the lone rower spent
bent double stubbornly
on keeping death at bay?
Why cast an eye?

Just stare
past the park-bencher
sitting in fast judgement
passing sentence on
this unrepentant
passerby.

Should I,
now paddling to my shins
in autumn, fill
this saddening confessional
with my processional of sins,
plead guilty still,

despair —
when dusk, grey lover
while hovering to cover
snowberry all virginal,
dare lower in to kiss
and tease too pleasing berberis?

MISS SHEEHAN AT HADRIAN'S VILLA

Miss Sheehan mild-eyed stood and stared
and staring back at her from the cool
cloistered waters of the pool
of Canapo saw childhood's cherub face
all shawled about in Limerick lace.

Under the Caryatides cold stony gaze
our spinster would she, think you, be ensnared
on sighting somewhat ruefully sideways
Mars marble buttocks or, full bared
a battling Amazon's bold breasts
and, strewn around abounding, there
remaindered, all the heavy ground where
clawing down antiquity still rests
a royal past enthroned deep in decay?

But weaving close by wheat-sheaves trooped
to charge the living, suddenly she stooped
from high relief, all smiles, and whipped away
a growing poppy, lopped off its flopping head
and prayed to God the old gods were dead
and buried forever and a day.

RESTING

After he had read
the ordinary lists
of the dying and the dead
I heard the gentle sound
of the old priest's hard words
echoing round
the sunlit church
with a feeling — quite absurd —
that if the body here is husk
as Father Tom insists,
I might be run aground,
I might have been
left somewhere in the lurch,
rather as between,
say, Rush and Lusk.

But not long after,
knocked flying from my perch
by a child's fists
I heard behind my back
a child's laughter.

And have I not seen
set aside
from the solemn-visaged tide
of the water-tight Camac
ten fishes in a jar;
and in the Devil's Glen
encountered hordes and herds
of men
with a very distant view of hell;
and not so far

from Chapelizod winked at mists
of midges weaving in the dusk
a wizard pattern
to adorn the tousled head
of that queenly slattern,
Anna Livia Plurabelle?

While now, in bed,
and if I never stirred
again I swear I saw a star
in flight down towards Shanganagh —
like a white, white bird.

Whatever way they felt, the Jews,
at the unusual phenomenon
of quails and manna
or proud Pharoah on
the quiver of old Aaron's rod,
now as I nod
I ponder on and muse
upon the oddity of God.

LEGEND

(Malvern 1978)

A snowy night in Hertfordshire,
(*Beginners, please*) I saw him there,
the rear of his high head, and saw
through evening windows whitening pride
poised over some rare book, refuelling
inferno or celestial fire,
your sage and guileful guide
could lesson Times, Izvestia, l'Aurore.

You may have heard of him before —
his street the street named strangely Synge,
for clue the house in Hatch Street — Shaw,
heard of some Irish actor fallen ill
in his Dilemma . . . (To tell
the truth, the fellow fell down flat
on the Haymarket stage,
dead drunk as Louis Dubedat).
Love, duty — Jinny Gwinny, what the hell,
you were the beauty of your age!

Of Malvern hard by Beacon Hill —
where brooding English feet once trod
to raise a blaze to whip the Spanish ships —
we know how Malvern's pretty pilgrimage
of plodders possibly in search of God
engage your badinage, old stager. Sage
all smiling on the Little Black Girl's lips
he still lives on who never could be still
while trippingly outwitting Avon's Will
in, say, You Never Can (or can you?) Tell.

Pretend for ending — by his bed
a lady, bending down to kiss the
head farewell that Epstein sculpted,
all curious callously enquired,
'*Whatever should it feel like, Barney — death*?
(Did woman ever pinch her punches!)
Make literary history,' she cried.
How well he might not have replied
and history he rendered up for dead.

But on a dying note, a fading breath —
no, not fed up, just sounding tired —
'*A new experience* . . .', he whispered.

Is history now satisfied?

ACHILL SOUND

Of one who claims that never has he grown
up yet — to have the Lord feel quite at home —
making of it his life philosophy,
did I but have the gift of prophesy
on Achill Sound as distant monks intone,
this one, I'd say, might crowing outgrow Rome.

A LINE TO LENINGRAD

ya rad vas vidyet, Leningrad —
da, ochen rad, I say it — glad,
and to have touched the holy hand
of Shostokovitch — in Ireland —
the hero hand that waved a wand
in music over Leningrad
and blood so beautiful, blood red.

Severe of face, your Puskin said.
Yet dancing snow in Leningrad
are smiles from all your million dead.

LOCH RI

The lake did seem
a peace within my reach,
all dream, ambition done
and wishing — faceless each;

till a lone tern fishing
suddenly swung
lunging with vicious grace
to peak his fish.

And the old worm turns
in the split brain
and the bitter wound comes
creeping back again.

HUNGER

Why did you haste away so soon, my love,
I left unwise with no regrets, my love,
for could the long way round be best, my love,
in childhood's wild and wasted wisdom — you —
to wait for baby buttercups, clover
and seaside heather, gliding waters over
sands wind-whitening over all things true,
your frightening hunger and God's hunger too?
Now is the flying feathered curlew you,
the curling cloud rounding tall Errigal,
your Donegal and all your North your breath,
and shall I daring grudge you death, my love?

On the death of the hunger-striker,
Joe McDonnell, on 8 July 1981.

AISLING

In the quiet of graves she moved,
old roses nodding courteously,
wraith wreathed in veils of memory,
a breathing waif in life I loved.

In silence stranded I see her there
gracing her cheek with one frail hand,
eyes darkly wondering where
she might in memory be.
                              'Stand
so sundown brushes back lost gold
into the keeping of your hair.'

'Fool chaffinch flitting in the firs
above us, be my witness, swear
that she my sculpt in shadow stirs,
and stirs to life my living here.'

What dreaming ever may be told
to men who cannot shed a tear,
to unbelieving men, why even mere
table-crumb for curs?
                              'Then start
no more in dread of that last cold
cold girdling, death, nor shall you hear
again that door's dull thud to part
us — host me still, dear shade, enfold
me, gentle ghost, forever hold
me close to your unfading heart.'

CONFITEOR

O dear my Lord, but what a tricky
cute and cunning customer in me
you have across your counter, one
eluding true communion's equity.

That you, you Three in One and One in Three,
could fail to see through me, could be
wide open to my wide-eyed bribery
or guiltily contrive—
you, Father, Holy Spirit and the Son—
to look the other way, conniving
at the filching and the fun
of taking all for free . . . say
which of us would thus betray,
pretending Satan's not alive!

O I can fake and I can fable,
I can fiddle, fib and fumble,
glibly gamble with you, Lord
(and tell me, boys, who better able!),
provide you do not grumble
that I blunt Saint Michael's sword,
lay not all my cards upon your table,
refusing me, accusing me
that I, I only ape humility,
in pride but feigning to be humble.

I myself with guiltless smile
myself beguiling, shall I you beguile!

FAUSTUS KELLY TO HIS MIRROR

'So what is left over now to be sold
but a half-cracked empty, a twisted
and kissless dry lecher the Innocents' blood
could not whiten, this sepulchre whited
in ageless decaying — so parrot your prayers,
unholy old joker, go mutter your creed.

'And what is left over — lead for gold.
That your metal had ever existed
to settle a bargain that never held good,
for how soon from the start was it blighted! —
and Hell is for playing patrician airs,
you fag-end old smoke of a guttersnipe breed.'

LUX IN TENEBRIS

(In Memory of Esmond Knight, Actor)

Blinded half-blind yet more blind
than one tapping his pavement staccato, unblessed
and, lest falling I fail, the furthest behind
a way guessed at, ferreting after the rest

all amiss, my mind but half in and half out
of itself, left a blurred broken sight,
stray feet I strayed after, feet shifting about
O this way and that — grey drainage of Night . . .

when adrift over Liffey — or Thames — far out
hung the Lodestar I knew of a sudden turned Bird
as it flew to me, Love-Bird and true living Ghost
is the Love-Breath all giving wrung free from the Word

forever to be our once-breathed-upon Host,
Word calling, calling the soundless shout
that pierces an ear long deaf as a post;
and close beside I hear the dear sigh

eternally there of the Passerby
yearning, falling, tumbling a Cross.
I try, thunderstruck, to cry out. I am dumb,
I am humbled. What Lucifer-lightning loss

made me wander wondering Who, this eye,
could it be — this Sun I was sundered from.

OMNIBUS

O little seductress
all rucksack, halfdressed —
a springtrousered buttock
a nipple tucked in —
O blessed skin-beauty
now entering in,

O lucky one luckless, for what can you know
of original sin,
of death's heavy duty,
sagged bowel and breast
of the grey-moustached hag

here beside herself now,
a bagful of envy — jest
ditched at wit's end?
O how can you know
when she will descend . . .
or you, with the rest!

SIN STRIP

(In memory of Honor Bright)

Blob now in fashion white-trousered and jacketed,
Summer-bloused offering in the late June air,
Tracking a racketing junior executive
Rounding our flowering Fitzwilliam Square,

As he slows up under lazy laburnum,
Stopped overhung by the red hawthorn,
Hungering hand up she lunges, the lurchers
Plunged each to each to bed-bargaining born.

Leadenly laden in the outworn action,
Dark deed done dead in a company car,
Hades in waiting, paid ecstacy's echo,
Light fading nightshades said — 'Night, Lucifer!'

VOX EX SENO

From this dark limbo dare I preach?
For Mummy,. was she never told?
Who else shall teach her, who else teach
her no such thing is heart of gold?

Did we not both endure a thirst
for other life as each to each
feeling we shared each other first?
I was no slip 'twixt cup and lip.

Please, was it mine or Mummy's fault
that breach, failure, far-flung Fall
of apple — Adam's madam, all
of us in passion's partnership?

Trapped, plucked in grappled row
of overreach to overthrow
our world of both, must I be cursed
dead fruit of Judas kiss and grin?

My others, trouble you to know
before our floating bubble burst,
not mine, nor first nor last, the sin,
not mine the double somersault;

I had been born a bit at least
of your forgotten God, my caul
no image torn from off the Beast —
Creation's part and part of all;

and if part human, part divine,
no sport am I for a rash ruse
to use for Mummy's loss and mine,
this last resort, to wound, to bruise,

flick, flush, freak out to burn — trash,
a tremble tumbling from a womb,
untrusted, brushed out blur of ash,
the dustbin fashioned for my tomb.

Ashes to ashes, dust to dust . . .
but never in time between for me
to suffer blush or lash of lust.
Conceived, I had been pleased to be.

SUMMER REFLECTION

(Westmeath — September 1980)

Fly-flicking cattle-tail, quiet byre,
old rattle-rumbling tractor on the road,
a bold hallo, slow smile, a long blank stare,
wild antic light on hay, on boyhood hair —

child careless of a frantic butterfly
at odds with air, aware less of God, of fire
and chaff and living grain, or of the load
of loss, of gain; again, that we must weep
for man by man enslaved, tied, chained
to a tired world that cannot sleep nor die
to mean things meaningless that man has craved
to hold, which, sold himself, he cannot keep . . .

In this small piece of Eden Saviour-saved,
still endlessly the stabled Babe will cry —
the lambkin calling on the straying sheep —
for a lost Paradise to be regained.

HURST CHURCHYARD

(to Elizabeth Anne 1894-1973, Priest)

Here lies Elizabeth so recently deceased —
But how on earth could woman be a priest!
If it be true the lady never mated,
Why, did she then deserve to be cremated!

THE LONG ROAD FROM LILLIPUT

1

Aye, there it was in Lilliput
The young lad spied I sprightly dancing.
Aye, put he lightning in his foot
Defiant up against the rest
With Rogha 'n Fhile, jig and reel,
And all the medals on his chest
With pride at springing toe and heel
Were brightly, manifestly prancing.

2

'O far far cry from Lilliput',
Cried he, the old lad, lightly lading
Dark porter down his deepest gut.
The gargle gurled to the dregs
He rose and roared, 'So here I come
Hobbling with one of two fine legs.'
And flung the aluminium
Aside, his wooden leg upgrading.

3

There by the lake at Lilliput,
Westmeath, white-laced and graced with reaching
Pen and cygnet, now I shut
My gob to lob across a stone
Or send it skimming with this tale
Of a lone dancer's first atone-
ment for the loss of Holy Grail.
Far better this than all your preaching.

QUESTIONNAIRE

Who, who shall save his face
in this oddly uneven race — confess —
towards the endlessness all play for save
the knave who having kept his straight, no less,
moreover optimistically grave,
will think to twist himself a place?

Shall they, the gay dogs and the strays,
the fast ones, the fairest —
who first and last in the two days
past us dared rarely slip their traces
or the deserving brave? Who best
can still their faces save?

Our enemy, will he that other I
whose guarded faith moves molehills see
straight the already burrowed course
he borrows just to force
ridiculously quick rebirth —
hollow victory from a crumbling earth?

Can she the wife, outstrip tonguetie
competitors and lick them out of shape,
then break the tape into eternity
with the usual woman's trick
of promising the Lord
a little more than lady can afford?

To-day outpaced by the holy hound
have we lost face, our proper places,
lost too much solid ground,
just failed the test
in failing to behave
and safely jailed ourselves before arrest?

Then, counting on no further graces
ever to count as blessed
again thiss little mound of dust,
lest we go broke
must we the besters best
to be among the Just?

And one test question for the rest
before they sleep, the other folk all dressed
up in their odd disguise
of the detesting sad ungodly-wise,
these — will they never see the Joke
deep deep in the dead Jester's eyes?

UNITY

Dear soul, whenever you may come upon the rest
that's missing, do reshape my body at its best —
aged thirty-three or thereabouts, or rising forty,
well before it stales into a dirty story
to regale you on our slippery seventh course —
not out of nothing nowhere, no, but nothing — no, sir —
less than springtimes we could never have been closer
in our bountiful renouncings prior divorce.

And don't you take all time, at any rate no longer
than to see our old headmaster, Science — wronger
and the same dead ringer for exactitudes —
pass blindly by belling at last an end of feuds
with quaint beliefs that charitably might leave room
for scholar ancients to squat swotting at Christ's tomb,
or — naming one — say Russell, game agnostic gnome,
to go along hobnobbing with the Pope of Rome.

CROSS TALK

'Himself on the Wood there,' says one,
'is surely the Son of His Mother,
a Man done undoing what's done,'
'He could be Himself', says another.

Said she, 'He's Himself is my own,
Himself only, born to be given,
bled whitest, white Bread of my bone,
red liveliest Wine for all living.'

FOR JUDAS

I

Good Friday — before
the crucial crosspoint
of the first Elevation
he ran like a hare
for King's Cross railway-station.

He turned coat and tail
trailing his kite high
over that hardest old Station —
the failure to fail
in our long crucifixion.

Turning a blind eye
on time out of joint
and this commemoration,
despairing, despair
he fled fearing conviction.

II

Stale kiss of self-sale
may click shut the gate
in betrayal, denying
the Fruit in the Core,
the rejected rejection.

But King may checkmate
the Pawn's haltered flight
to that Marble-eyed eying
us each out of sight —
each back-sliding cross-section

in the long run part
of His racing heart —
yet may pluck from the flying
dust of apostate
the Spring-flower, resurrection.

ULTIMA THULE

With rubbertipped stick and shortfall of breath
age let me accept — no leisurely stroll
but a lumbering on to my small lawn of death
there to dig and to delve for a newborn soul.

But what blessed spirit in shape of a bird
alights here beside me so brighteyed winking?
Peck, hop, Featherhead, and no testy word
shall check your pert chirrup, shall stop your quick whistling.

Man, pest of mankind, his own Satan, Lord save
him and love let us have for all creatures living.
For Man too, O Lord, then love let us have
so darling my Bird may go wing away singing.

NUMBER ONE

Star dressing-room —
my prison and my home,
my salvation and my doom,
my Calvary, my Rome.

BETWEEN THE ACTS
(for Father Leonard O.P.)

Whatever about words, facts,
We still may aim
for light between the acts,
at intervals proclaim
no more than that we each,
though very much the same,
can be divinely different
and differently reach
toward the One Magnificent.